TOP 10 AMERICAN MEN SPRINTERS

Ron Knapp

SPORTS TOP 10

Enslow Publishers, Inc.

44 Fadem Road   PO Box 38
Box 699   Aldershot
Springfield, NJ 07081 Hants GU12 6BP
USA   UK
http://www.enslow.com

Library of Congress Cataloging-in-Publication Data

Knapp, Ron.
    Top 10 American men sprinters / Ron Knapp.
       p. cm. — (Sports top 10)
    Includes bibliographical references (p. 46) and index.
    Summary: Highlights the lives and careers of ten great American sprinters,
including Henry Carr, Bob Hayes, Jim Hines, Michael Johnson, Carl Lewis,
Bobby Joe Morrow, Jesse Owens, Charlie Paddock, Tommie Smith, and Eddie
Tolan.
    ISBN 0-7660-1074-0
    1. Runners (Sports)—United States—Biography—Juvenile literature.
2. Runners (Sports)—Rating of—United States—Juvenile literature.
3. Sprinting—United States—Juvenile literature. [1. Runners (Sports)
2. Track and field athletes.] I. Title. II. Series.
GV1061.14K63   1999
796.42'2'092273—dc21
   [B]   98-25725
                                             CIP
                                           AC

To Our Readers:
All Internet addresses in this book were active and appropriate when we
went to press. Any comments or suggestions can be sent by e-mail to
Comments@enslow.com or to the address on the back cover.

Illustration Credits: Abilene Christian University, pp. 27, 29; AP/Wide
World Photos, pp. 6, 9, 11, 13, 15, 17, 18, 21, 22, 25, 30, 38, 41, 42, 45;
Courtesy Gerald R. Ford Library, p. 33; Courtesy University of Southern
California, pp. 34, 37.

Cover Illustration: AP/Wide World Photos

Cover Description: Michael Johnson, 1996 Olympic gold medalist, 200-
meter and 400-meter dashes.

Interior Design: Richard Stalzer

CONTENTS

Introduction

THE FASTEST MAN IN THE WORLD. What a title. What a goal. Athletes have been racing one another for thousands of years, but formal track competitions did not become organized until late in the nineteenth century. Up to that point, no one was ever sure who the world's quickest sprinter was.

Since the modern Olympic Games began in 1896, the sports world has been able to focus on competition featuring the fastest sprinters on the planet. The first gold-medal winner in the 100-meter dash was Thomas Burke, an American who clocked 12.0 seconds. The first winner of the 200-meter dash, added to the Olympics in 1900, was another American, John Tewksbury, at 22.2 seconds.

World-class sprinters now cover 100 meters in less than 10 seconds. By the 1984 Olympics, the top two finishers in the 200-meter dash both had broken 20 seconds.

Why do sprint times keep falling? Athletes today train longer, harder, and smarter. Today's athletes do not have to worry about holding down regular jobs. They also have the benefits of better knowledge of nutrition, training methods, and the workings of the human body. And years ago, track surfaces were made of small stones called cinders. It is much easier to blaze across today's high-tech synthetic tracks.

Of course, there have been other changes in the world of sprinting in the past century. Even though Olympic races have always been measured in meters, many races in the United States used to be measured in yards, a slightly shorter span. Today the sport of track and field in the United States follows the rest of the world in using meters.

Successful male sprinters today are rich people. In the old days, that was not the case. In the 1920s, Olympian Eddie Tolan could not earn the money to go to medical school.

Thirty years ago, Bob Hayes gave up track so that he could become a professional football player. Today, endorsement contracts, appearance fees, and prize money have made millionaires of athletes like Carl Lewis and Michael Johnson.

When the modern Olympics began, all of the sprinters were white. Today almost all of them are black. The first great African-American sprinters, like Tolan and Jesse Owens, seemed happy just to have the chance to run. Later athletes, like Tommie Smith, protested strongly against racial discrimination and prejudice.

Not everyone may agree with *our* list of the ten top sprinters. But despite the differences in race, income, style, training methods, and the times in which they lived, all the men in this book had the same goal. Each wanted to be recognized as the fastest human on the planet. And for a few days, or a few years, that is what they were.

OLYMPIC CAREER STATISTICS

Athlete	100-meter	200-meter	400-meter	4 x 100 R	4 x 400 R
HENRY CARR		Gold (1964)			Gold (1964)
BOB HAYES	Gold (1964)			Gold (1964)	
JIM HINES	Gold (1968)			Gold (1968)	
MICHAEL JOHNSON		Gold (1996)	Gold (1996)		Gold (1992)
CARL LEWIS	Gold (1984) Gold (1988)	Gold (1984) Silver (1988)		Gold (1984) Gold (1992)	
BOBBY JOE MORROW	Gold (1956)	Gold (1956)		Gold (1956)	
JESSE OWENS	Gold (1936)	Gold (1936)		Gold (1936)	
CHARLIE PADDOCK	Gold (1920)	Silver (1920) Silver (1924)		Gold (1920)	
TOMMIE SMITH		Gold (1968)			
EDDIE TOLAN	Gold (1932)	Gold (1932)			

R=Relay

HENRY CARR

Sprinter Henry Carr shows off the gold medal he won in the 200-meter dash during the 1964 Olympics.

WHEN IT CAME TIME for the 1964 Olympics, Henry Carr could not seem to get serious until it really counted.

Even though he held the world record in the 200-meter dash at 20.2 seconds, he ran so poorly at the United States trials that he finished fourth behind Paul Drayton, Richard Stebbins, and Bob Hayes. With each country's team limited to three athletes in each event, Carr was in trouble.

Luckily for him, the American coaches had confidence in his ability to deliver when it counted. Carr was entered in the 200 ahead of Hayes, who was already the favorite for the 100.

In the Olympic preliminaries, Carr remained laid back and relaxed. Although he advanced to the finals, he was beaten by Drayton, who recorded a best time of 20.5.

But Carr did not seem to be worried. Instead, he enjoyed being in Tokyo, Japan. The 1964 Olympics were the first ever held in Asia. Carr and many of the other athletes enjoyed visiting the various tourist attractions. He and Drayton visited a geisha house.

Drayton loved it. But Carr was not impressed by the service, and he did not like the Japanese food. "Yeah," he said. "They fed us seaweed."[1]

Soon it was time to forget about the attractions and the exotic food. Drayton and Carr faced each other in the final of the 200-meter dash. Drayton did not surprise anybody when he took an early lead.

But then Carr came alive. For the first time since the two men had begun dueling each other weeks before in the American trials, he poured it on. Carr quickly passed

Drayton and was leading by a yard by the time they came around the turn. Then he steadily built his lead over Drayton and Trinidad's Edwin Roberts. Carr's time was 20.36. He was .18 seconds and more than four feet ahead of Drayton. He beat Roberts by .27 seconds to earn the gold medal.

Carr had one event left—the 4 x 400-meter relay. His American teammates—Ollan Cassell, Michael Larrabee, and Ulis Williams—had built up a lead by the time he took the baton.

At first, Carr looked as if he was in trouble. Runners from the United Kingdom and Trinidad began to close on him. But just before they caught him, Carr began to accelerate, faster and faster. When he crossed the finish line, he was ahead by five meters. The Americans' time was incredible—3:00.7. They had smashed the world record by 1.5 seconds.

Larrabee was amazed by Carr's performance. "Hank could run 400 meters in 44 flat," he said. "Trouble is he's lazy." Larrabee knew what he was talking about. He had just won gold in the 400 himself with a time of 45.1 seconds.

But Carr said he was satisfied with two gold medals. "Why should I run 400 meters?" he asked. "I'm the world's best at 200. I'm not greedy."[2]

HENRY CARR

BORN: November 27, 1942, Detroit, Michigan.

COLLEGE: Arizona State University.

MEDALS: Gold medal winner, 200-meter dash, 1964 Olympics; Gold medal winner, 4 x 400-meter relay, 1964 Olympics.

HONORS: Inducted into the USA Track and Field Hall of Fame, 1987.

Lunging forward, Henry Carr crosses the finish line ahead of the competition. Carr won the 200-meter dash with a time of 20.36 seconds in the 1964 Olympics.

Internet Address

http://www.usatf.org/athletes/hof/carr.shtml

Bob Hayes

Bob Hayes Was A Slow Kid. When he was a baby, it took him a long time to learn to walk. When he was a little older, it seemed to take him forever to do his chores around the house.

As he grew up, Hayes did not appear to have the body of a runner. His ankles were thin, and he was pigeon-toed—his toes pointed inward instead of out. His upper body was well developed. He looked strong and powerful. Most runners are thin and sleek; Bob Hayes looked like a football player.

And that is how he got his start in athletics. He was a star running back on the Gilbert High School football team in Jacksonville, Florida. Once at practice, just for fun, he challenged the school's fastest sprinter to a race. When Hayes whipped him, the track coach convinced Hayes to join the team the following spring. In his first 100-yard dash, he clocked 10.1 seconds. Before he graduated, he was down to 9.6.

Hayes was fast, but he still did not look like a sprinter. "My 'style' . . . was to run knock-kneed and pigeon-toed . . . and I often spiked myself when I ran," he said.[1]

At Florida A&M University, Hayes was again a football star and, despite his size and his build, a nationally known track star. He became the first man to hit 9.1 seconds in the 100-yard dash. He also set world records in the 70-yard dash (6.9 seconds) and 60-yard dash (5.9 seconds). The muscular sprinter seemed to pick up speed with each step. Hayes was once timed at 26.9 miles per hour!

At the 1964 Olympics in Tokyo, Japan, he was almost stopped from winning a gold medal in the 100-meter dash

BOB HAYES

Bob Hayes celebrates after the United States won the
4 x 100-meter relay gold medal at the 1964 Olympics.

by Joe Frazier, a gold-medal-winning boxer and a future heavyweight champ. When Frazier took a stick of gum from Hayes's gym bag, Hayes' left shoe fell out. At the track just before the race, Hayes had to borrow a shoe. It was a cold, wet day, and the track was in terrible shape, but, as Hayes said later, "I didn't come all the way to Tokyo to lose."[2] He finished in 10.06 seconds to tie the world record, two meters and two-tenths of a second ahead of the other sprinters. He handed his medal to his mother and said, "Here's your gold, mother dear, just like I promised you."[3]

Six days later he was the anchor man on the United States' 4 x 100-meter relay team. When he got the baton, he was two meters behind the leader. "The runners . . . were kicking up cinders off their spikes, and the cinders were burning my eyes," he said. "Suddenly I started passing guys like they were standing still . . . I knew I was moving faster than I had ever moved before." Hayes won the race by three meters. For his 100-meter leg, the time was 8.9 seconds! A writer called it "the most astonishing sprint of all time."[4]

At the Olympics, Jesse Owens, the star of the 1936 Olympics, told Hayes to give up football and stick with track. "I'll think about it," Hayes answered, "but I love football, Mr. Owens, and there's an opportunity there for me to earn a living in the future."[5]

Later in 1964, Bullet Bob Hayes signed a contract with the Dallas Cowboys of the National Football League. As a flanker and a punt-returner, he helped lead the team to a Super Bowl victory in 1972. Hayes played for Dallas until 1974.

Unfortunately, Hayes was arrested for selling cocaine in 1978 and served ten months in prison. After that, he worked hard to put his life in order. He returned to college and graduated from Florida A&M in 1994 with a degree in elementary education.

BOB HAYES

BORN: December 20, 1942, Jacksonville, Florida.

HIGH SCHOOL: Gilbert High School, Jacksonville, Florida.

COLLEGE: Florida A&M.

MEDALS: Gold medal winner, 100-meter dash, 1964 Olympics; Gold medal winner 4 x 100-meter relay, 1964 Olympics.

HONORS: Selected to NFL All-Pro Team, 1966; Member of Dallas Cowboys Super Bowl VI championship team; Inducted into USA Track and Field Hall of Fame, 1976.

Bob Hayes (center) after receiving his gold medal for the 100-meter dash.

Internet Address

http://www.usatf.org/athletes/hof/hayes_bob.shtml

JIM HINES

JIM HINES RUSHED FOR 869 YARDS and scored 13 touchdowns for the McClymonds High School football team in Oakland, California. But after graduation, he decided to focus on track at Texas Southern University. He wanted to be the fastest man on earth.

Steadily, Hines lowered his times. In 1967, he tied a world record with 5.9 seconds in the 60-yard dash. Just before the 1968 Olympics in Mexico City, he became the first man to run the 100-meter dash in less than ten seconds. He did it in 9.95!

In the Olympic 100-meter dash, for the first time all the finalists were black. That was especially significant, because sprinter Tommie Smith had urged black athletes to stay away to protest racism in America. Hines had argued that African Americans should compete at the Olympics to show their skill to the world. Finally, the black athletes decided to compete.

Hines had always been one of the fastest starters in racing. Sometimes, in fact, he was disqualified for leaving the blocks too soon. But at the 1968 Olympics, he was perfect. After a beautiful start, he was even with teammate Charles Greene before pulling away at the 70-meter mark to win by a meter. His time: once again, 9.95 seconds. "It was my greatest race," he said. "The greatest thing that will ever happen to me."[1]

Hines had reached his goal. "The Olympic 100-meter dash decides who is the world's fastest human," he said.[2] Not only did he have his gold medal; he also had a world record that would stand for another fifteen years.

JIM HINES

Baton in hand, Jim Hines finishes ahead of the pack. Hines anchored the United States team to victory in the 4 x 100-meter relay during the 1968 Olympics.

In the finals of the 4 x 100-meter relay, the Americans were in trouble when Hines, the anchor man, finally got his turn. Poor baton passes had kept them in third place, five feet behind the leader. Hines took the baton and took off. He sailed past the Cuban and French sprinters to clinch another gold medal. The relay team clocked 38.24 seconds, another world record.

Despite his accomplishments, Hines received little notice from the press. Most of the attention was focused on Smith and John Carlos, African-American athletes who gave a black-gloved salute during the medal ceremony for the 200-meter dash. All the accomplishments of the American runners were overshadowed by that protest against racism.

Hines was not pleased. A shoe manufacturer backed out on an endorsement contract with him. "They felt we were all in on the protest," he said. "Everybody did." Hines had been drafted by the National Football League's Miami Dolphins. If not for the protest, he said, "I would have tripled my money from the Dolphins . . . . That gesture cost me a total of $2 million."[3] Hines was cut by the Dolphins after just one season.

But more than the money, Hines was upset that his feats in the 1968 Olympics received very little popular recognition. "It's hard not to think about it," he said years later. "Especially when people can't even remember you."[4]

JIM HINES

BORN: September 10, 1946, Dumas, Arkansas.

HIGH SCHOOL: McClymonds High School, Oakland, California.

COLLEGE: Texas Southern University.

MEDALS: Gold medal winner, 100-meter dash, 1968 Olympics; Gold medal winner, 4 x 100-meter relay, 1968 Olympics.

HONORS: Inducted into the USA Track and Field Hall of Fame, 1979.

Jim Hines (#279) ran the 100-meter dash at the 1968 Olympics in 9.95 seconds. That set a new world record, and for the time being he was the world's fastest man.

Internet Address

http://www.usatf.org/athletes/hof/hines.shtml

MICHAEL JOHNSON

At the 1996 Olympics in Atlanta, Georgia, Michael Johnson set an Olympic record in the 400-meter dash.

HE WAS ONLY TEN YEARS OLD, but Michael Johnson has never forgotten what it was like to win his first race—a 50-yard dash. "I remember the exhilaration that came from knowing that I was the FASTEST!"[1]

But when he was growing up in Dallas, Texas, school-work was the most important thing in Johnson's life. His mother, Ruby Johnson, was a teacher who even made her children do schoolwork during summer vacations. Michael did so well in school that he was usually in classes for gifted students. He did not go out for track during his first year of high school because he wanted to concentrate on his studies.

After modest success as a sprinter during his junior and senior years, Johnson earned a scholarship to Baylor University. It was there that Johnson, under the guidance of his long-time coach, Clyde Hart, began pushing himself to the limit to be one of the world's fastest sprinters.

Observers were quick to notice Johnson's unusual stride. "My form is all wrong," he admitted.[2] Instead of bending slightly and taking long strides, Johnson keeps his body straight and takes short strides just like his hero, Jesse Owens. It's unusual, but it works. As he admits, "I was a sleek, powerful machine. A perfect machine."[3]

Johnson was expected to be in the running for a spot on the United States team in the 400-yard dash for the 1988 Seoul Olympics, but before the United States Trials he suffered a stress fracture in his left fibula (a bone in his lower leg) and was unable to advance to the final. During the next two years, he focused his energy on winning NCAA titles on his college track team.

Four years later, he lowered his best time in the 200 to

19.79 seconds, just before the start of the 1992 Barcelona Olympics. While competing in Europe prior to the Olympics, he was hit by food poisoning, losing six pounds and two weeks of training. He was not strong enough even to qualify for the final. However, he recovered in time to help set a world-record time of 2:55.74 in the 4 x 400-meter relay.

After two Olympic disappointments, Johnson set his sights on the 1996 Olympic Games in Atlanta, Georgia. He decided he would run both the 200 and 400. No man had ever won both events in the same Olympics. Olympic officials rescheduled the competition so that he would not have to run rounds of both events on the same day.

A month before the Olympics, he clocked 19.66 in the 200, erasing a world record that had stood for seventeen years. He was healthy and ready. When he arrived in Atlanta, there was no doubt about his goal—he was wearing customized gold running shoes.

In his first event, the 400-meter dash, he won a gold medal and set an Olympic record of 43.49. Two days later, he was back on the track for the final of the 200-meter dash. The huge crowd was silent as the sprinters got into position. "This is the one you want," Johnson told himself.[4]

The gun sounded, and Johnson stumbled slightly. But the gold shoes started to fly. "I knew coming off the curve it was faster than I've ever run," he said. "It was over."[5]

When he crossed the finish line, he glanced at the clock. 19.32! Johnson had cut .34 off his own world record! "My arms flew open in disbelief and everything dissolved in a rush of camera flashes, cheers, and the powerful sense that I had done something truly special," Johnson remembered.[6]

Records for dashes are almost always lowered by a few thousandths of a second. Johnson had chopped off more than one third of a second! Fans could only wonder: What if he had not stumbled at the start?

Michael Johnson

Born: September 13, 1967, Dallas, Texas.

High School: Skyline High School, Dallas, Texas.

College: Baylor University.

Medals: Gold medal winner, 4 x 400-meter relay, 1992 Olympics; Gold medal winner, 200-meter dash, 1996 Olympics; Gold medal winner, 400-meter dash, 1996 Olympics.

Honors: Holds Olympic record for 400-meter dash, 43.49; Holds world record for 200-meter dash, 19.32; First man to win both the 200-meter, and 400-meter dash in the same Olympic Games.

In 1996, Johnson became the first man to win a gold medal in both the 200-meter and 400-meter dash in the same Olympic games. Winning on home soil made the victory even sweeter.

Internet Address

http://www.usatf.org/athletes/bios/johnsonm.shtml

CARL LEWIS

USA

Atlanta 1996

2374

Carl Lewis is one of the greatest athletes in Olympic history. Aside from being a legendary sprinter, he also won gold medals in the long-jump competition in four consecutive Olympics.

CARL LEWIS

WHEN HE WAS EIGHT YEARS OLD, Carl Lewis watched his cousin play football. When one of the players was hit hard and had trouble getting up, the coach screamed, "Get up! Be a man!" Lewis was horrified. "Right then I knew the sport wasn't for me."[1]

Instead, the little boy turned to track. At first, he just made sand castles in the long-jump pit with his little sister, Carol, while his parents, William and Evelyn, coached high school teams in Willingboro, New Jersey. Later, the children organized their own "track meets" at home, using chairs for hurdles and a sand pile for a long-jump pit. Usually Carol beat Carl. Even though he was older, "She was bigger than I was," he said. "Everybody was bigger than I was."[2]

Lewis was short and skinny until he was fifteen. Then he hit a growth spurt that was so rapid doctors put him on crutches for a month while his body adjusted. A year later he was sprinting 10.6 seconds in the 100 meters and jumping 23 feet, 9 inches in the long jump.

When he was only twenty-two, Lewis won the long jump and both sprints, the 100- and 200-meter dashes, at the 1983 World Track and Field Championships. By then, he had already set a goal: "This may sound funny, but my goal is to be the best of all-time."[3]

At the 1984 Olympics in Los Angeles, Sam Graddy was leading Lewis with only twenty meters to go in the 100. "Then I saw him out of the corner of my eye," Graddy remembered.[4] Lewis zipped past like he was on fire. He won the race by eight feet, hitting 28 miles per hour as he passed the finish line at 9.99 seconds. The 200 was a different story—with the same result. Lewis took an early lead, then had to hold off Kirk Baptiste to win by a meter and a half at 19.8.

Lewis also took the long-jump competition. When he anchored the victorious United States team in the 4 x 100-meter relay, his gold medal total hit four, the same total in the same events as Jesse Owens in 1936.

When William Lewis died in 1987, his youngest son put his 100-meter Olympic gold medal in the casket. "I want you to have this because it was your favorite event," he said. Then he turned to his mother and said, "Don't worry, I'll get another one."[5]

That's just what he did at the 1988 Olympics in Seoul, Korea. When Ben Johnson, the apparent winner, was disqualified after testing positive for steroids, Lewis's world-record time of 9.93 took gold. He also took the long jump and again anchored the winning 4 x 100-meter relay team.

Three years later, when he was thirty, Lewis met Leroy Burrell, the new 100-meter record-holder, at the 1991 World Track and Field Championships in Tokyo. It was a very fast race. "I'll bet four people broke the world record for 50 meters," Lewis said. "I felt great at 60, and I still was about fifth." Then he exploded. "He passed us like we were standing still," Burrell said. His time: 9.86, another world record. "The best race of my life. The best technique, the fastest. And I did it at 30."[6]

But Carl Lewis was not finished yet. His incredible 8.8-second anchor leg on the 4 x 100-meter relay gave the Americans another victory in the 1992 Barcelona Olympics. He took the long jump there and again at the 1996 Games in Atlanta, when he was thirty-five! He was the only Olympic long-jump gold-medal winner from 1984 to 1996.

Mel Rose, an Olympic coach, said, "Carl is the greatest athlete I have ever seen, and he proves it again and again."[7]

CARL LEWIS

BORN: July 1, 1961, Birmingham, Alabama.

HIGH SCHOOL: Willingboro High School, Willingboro, New Jersey.

COLLEGE: University of Houston.

MEDALS: Gold medal winner, 100-meter dash, 1984, 1988
Olympics; Gold medal winner, 200-meter dash, 1984
Olympics; Silver medal winner, 200-meter dash, 1988
Olympics; Gold medal winner, 4 x 100-meter relay, 1984,
1992 Olympics; Gold medal winner, long jump, 1984, 1988,
1992, 1996 Olympics.

HONORS: Sullivan Award Winner, 1981. Holds record for most
World Championship titles, 8.

Overcome with emotion, Carl Lewis celebrates the United States'
triumph in the 4 x 100-meter relay at the 1992 Olympics in
Barcelona, Spain.

Internet Address

http://www.usatf.org/athletes/bios/lewis.shtml

BOBBY JOE MORROW

WHEN BOBBY JOE MORROW LOOKED for a college, he was not just interested in a place where he could run track. He also wanted a place where he would receive a strong religious education. Morrow turned down scholarships from several major colleges to attend Abilene Christian College, a school operated by the Church of Christ.

The colleges were interested in Morrow because he had been a star in football, basketball, and track at high school in San Benito, Texas. Under the guidance of Jake Watson, his coach, Morrow won two state championships in the 100-yard dash. When he was a senior, he also took the 220. For the rest of his career, Morrow gave Watson the credit for making him a world-class sprinter.

When Morrow was a freshman at Abilene Christian, his best time in the 100-yard dash was 9.4 seconds, just a tenth of a second off the world record. When he was a sophomore, he won thirty-six 100s and lost only one—to Dave Sime. Morrow was already a dedicated athlete, but he hated to lose, and the loss made him work even harder. Besides hours of vigorous workouts every day, he also observed a strict diet and never touched tobacco or alcohol. He also made sure to get at least ten to eleven hours of sleep every night. On the track, he said, the trick was to be relaxed and confident. "Whatever success I have had is due to being so perfectly relaxed that I can feel my jaw muscles wiggle."[1]

Morrow got even with Sime early in 1956 when he beat him by two yards in an important track meet in Bakersfield, California. Then Morrow began concentrating all his energy on the coming Olympic Games in Melbourne, Australia.

Bobby Joe Morrow, of Abilene Christian College, practices for an upcoming meet. Morrow was a dedicated athlete.

BOBBY JOE MORROW

But just when he should have been doing some of his toughest training, Morrow got sick. In fact, he lost twenty pounds waiting for the Olympics. It looked as if he was in trouble. He was weak and out of shape.

As soon as his health improved, Morrow went back to work. When he got to Melbourne, he was ready. In the 100-meter preliminaries, he tied the Olympic record of 10.3 seconds. Then, in the final, he stormed out to a quick lead, and held on to beat American teammate W. Thane Baker.

But in taking the 100-meter gold medal, he suffered a slight groin pull. When he showed up for the 200-meter prelims, he was wearing a bandage on his left thigh. The fans wondered whether the injury might even keep him from competing. They shouldn't have worried. Halfway through the race he took command. Morrow sprinted his way to another gold medal and an Olympic record time of 20.75 seconds.

But Morrow was not finished. He anchored the United States 4 x 100-meter relay, which set a world record of 39.5 seconds. That victory made him the first American since Jesse Owens in 1936 to win three gold medals in the same Olympic Games.

After the 1956 Olympics and then his graduation from Abilene Christian, Morrow worked hard to stay in shape for the 1960 Games in Rome. He lowered his 100-yard time to 9.4 seconds, which tied the world record. In 1957, he was named the winner of the James E. Sullivan Memorial Award as the nation's best amateur athlete.

Unfortunately, despite his dedication, his times began to fall. By 1960, Bobby Joe Morrow was not even fast enough to make the American Olympic team.

BOBBY JOE MORROW

BORN: October 15, 1935, Harlingen, Texas.

HIGH SCHOOL: San Benito High School, San Benito, Texas.

COLLEGE: Abilene Christian College.

MEDALS: Gold medal winner, 100-meter dash, 1956 Olympics, Gold medal winner, 200-meter dash, 1956 Olympics, Gold medal winner, 4 x 100-meter relay, 1956 Olympics.

HONORS: Inducted into USA Track and Field Hall of Fame, 1975; Inducted into U.S. Olympic Hall of Fame, 1989.

Bobby Joe Morrow (left) discusses matters with Coach Oliver Jackson. In 1957, Morrow won the Sullivan Award as the nation's top amateur athlete.

Internet Address

http://www.usatf.org/athletes/hof/morrow.shtml

JESSE OWENS

Anchoring the American team, Jesse Owens takes the baton from teammate Frank Wykoff.

YOUNG JAMES CLEVELAND OWENS loved to run, but he didn't always have time. Coming from a poor African-American family, he had to spend a good deal of time working. When he was just six years old, he began picking cotton in rural Alabama. The family soon moved to Cleveland, Ohio, where he loaded trains, delivered groceries, and worked in a shoe-repair shop.

When a teacher mistakenly called him "Jesse," he was too shy to correct her. From then on, that is what everybody except his family called him. Another teacher, Charlie Riley, was amazed when he timed the boy running a 60-yard dash in gym class. Owens was so fast that Riley invited him to come out for the track team. Since the speedy youngster had to work after school, the teacher brought him in early every morning to practice.

Years later, Owens explained his running style: "I let my feet spend as little time on the ground as possible. From the air, fast down, and from the ground, fast up."[1]

When he was just an eighth grader, Owens ran the 100-yard dash in 9.9. He also long-jumped 23 feet. As a senior at Cleveland East Technical High School, he tied the world record for the 100, covering the distance in 9.4 seconds.

Running for Ohio State University in the Big Ten Championships on May 25, 1935, Owens had an unbeliev-able afternoon. First, he again tied the 100-yard world record, at 9.4 seconds. Then, during the next forty-five minutes, he set five world records. His long jump of 26 feet, 8 1/2 inches, was six inches longer than had ever been done before. He won the 220-yard dash in 20.3 seconds, also getting credit for the 200-meter dash. When he did 22.6 in the 220-yard low hurdles, his time was a record in that event and the 200-meter hurdles.

But it was Owens's performance at the 1936 Berlin Olympics that made him a legend. In the 100-meter dash final, he took an early lead and managed to hold off Ralph Metcalfe by a meter, with a time of 10.3 seconds. Even though it was raining, he won the 200-meter dash in 20.7 seconds, five meters ahead of teammate Mack Robinson.

He was also the lead runner on the American team that took the 4 x 100-meter relay in a world-record time of 39.8 seconds. And between runs, he also won a thrilling duel with Germany's Luz Long for first place in the long jump with 26 feet, 5 1/2 inches. Owens went home with four gold medals. More important, he had embarrassed German leader Adolf Hitler, who had claimed that the German athletes were of a superior race.

His accomplishments made some Americans think about the legal discrimination then existing against African Americans. "Since we are all Americans," Owens said, "Negroes should have a chance in every sport. Certainly the showing of Negroes in track events shows that if they have half a chance, they produce the goods."[2]

Even with his fame, it was not always easy for Owens to make a living after the 1936 Olympics. For a few months he appeared in a variety of exhibitions. "He ran against cars, trucks, dogs, and baseball players with a head start. He ran against anything and anybody, anywhere, and when there were no contestants, he ran just to please the customers."[3]

Owens spent decades speaking to thousands of young people, encouraging them to work hard and excel in athletics and all other fields. In 1976, United States President Gerald Ford awarded him the Medal of Freedom, the highest civilian honor bestowed by the United States.

Jesse Owens

BORN: September 12, 1913, Danville, Alabama.

DIED: March 31, 1980.

HIGH SCHOOL: Cleveland East Technical High School, Cleveland, Ohio.

COLLEGE: Ohio State University.

MEDALS: Gold medal winner, 100-meter dash, 1936 Olympics; Gold medal winner, 200-meter dash, 1936 Olympics, Gold medal winner, 4 x 100-meter relay, 1936 Olympics; Gold medal winner, long jump, 1936 Olympics.

HONORS: Broke 5 world records in one afternoon at Big Ten Championships, May 25, 1935; Inducted into USA Track and Field Hall of Fame, 1974; Received the Presidential Medal of Freedom, 1976; Inducted into the U.S. Olympic Hall of Fame, 1983.

More than just a great athlete, Jesse Owens became an American hero. He is shown here with President Gerald Ford after receiving the Presidential Medal of Freedom.

Internet Address

http://www.usatf.org/athletes/hof/owens.shtml

CHARLIE PADDOCK

With his trademark leap, Charlie Paddock crosses the finish line.

CHARLIE PADDOCK

CHARLIE PADDOCK WAS SUCH A SICKLY BABY that his parents moved him to sunny southern California. The move seemed to work. Charlie grew into a healthy, speedy teenager with a very unusual running style.

"From the side Charlie looked as though he were running in a sitting position," said a college friend. "His knees and feet were always out front."[1] The unique style did the trick. On April 3, 1921, he set or tied five world records—100 meters (10.4 seconds), 200 meters (21.6), 300 meters (33.8), 100 yards (9.6), and 200 yards (20.2).

Paddock was the first athlete to be known as The World's Fastest Human. That reputation made him famous and a friend to the biggest movie stars of the 1920s. His newspaper columns about his running exploits were read by millions.

At the 1920 Olympics in Antwerp, Belgium, Paddock was just behind Morris Kinsey as they neared the finish of the 100-meter dash. "I drove my spikes into the soft cinders and felt my foot give way as I sprang forward in a final jump for the tape," he said. He won by a foot in 10.8 seconds. "I thrilled to the greatest moment I felt that I should ever know."[2]

In fact, Paddock was so thrilled he stayed out late that night celebrating. He was so tired the next day he ran out of steam in the 200-meter final. Allen Woodring passed him for the gold medal. After the race, Woodring was surprised; he was convinced that Paddock had lost on purpose.

There was no chance of that. Paddock loved to win. He also loved his trademark leap. About twelve feet before the end of a sprint, he would throw himself through the air, with his arms stuck out almost like wings. When he flew over the finish line, the photographers were always there. Many coaches tried to convince him to simply run across the finish line like everybody else, but he would not. Maybe the leap did not really improve his time, he said, but it gave him something to look forward to at the end of a race.

Paddock did not get a chance to leap in his other Olympic race in 1920. Since he was the first man in the American 4 x 100-meter relay team, he had to hand off the baton. The team took gold, setting a world record of 42.2 seconds.

In 1924, Paddock felt discouraged about his chances of winning the 200-meter dash at the Paris Olympics. But the night before the race, a friend, the famous actress Mary Pickford, told him, "If you believe in yourself, you will win." He would have, too, if he had not turned around just before his final leap to see whether anybody was gaining on him. As he slowed slightly to look, Jackson Scholz blitzed by.

Paddock returned to the Amsterdam Olympics in 1928, but could not qualify for any finals. "I didn't have a thing left . . . " he said. "It must be age. My old kick isn't there."[3]

But Paddock's fastest time in the 100 meters (10.2) stood as a world record for another twenty-two years. When he died in the crash of a military plane during World War II, he was still the "world's fastest human." His time was not bested until 1950, when Panama's Lloyd LaBeach cut off a tenth of a second.

CHARLIE PADDOCK

BORN: November 8, 1900, Gainesville, Texas.

DIED: July 21, 1943.

COLLEGE: University of Southern California.

MEDALS: Gold medal winner, 100-meter dash, 1920 Olympics; Gold medal winner, 4 x 100-meter relay, 1920 Olympics; Silver medal winner, 200-meter dash, 1920, 1924 Olympics.

HONORS: Inducted into USA Track and Field Hall of Fame, 1976.

Enjoying time away from competition, Paddock hurdles with some friends. Sadly, Paddock was killed in action during World War II.

Internet Address

http://www.usatf.org/athletes/hof/paddock.shtml

TOMMIE SMITH

In one of the most controversial moments in sports history, Tommie Smith and John Carlos raised their fists on the medal stand in a protest of racial inequality.

THE WALL IN THE SAN JOSE STATE COLLEGE GYM was just a few feet past the end of the court. When he drove in for lay-ups, Tommie Smith was usually going so fast he could not stop before slamming into the wall. It hurt. It helped make him tired of basketball. Besides, there was another sport he liked better. Smith switched to track.

The switch was a great idea. In 1965, he tied the world record of 20.0 seconds for the straightaway 200-meter dash. A year later, he lowered it to 19.5 and set a new mark for the 200-meter on a curved track, at 20.0. That same year he anchored the first relay team to break three minutes for the 4 x 400-meter relay. They did it in 2:59.6. In 1967, he set two more world records—400 meters (44.5 seconds) and 440 yards (44.8 seconds).

Everybody agreed that his steady acceleration in races was exciting to watch. When he speeded up, reporters said he was switching into "Tommie-jet gear."[1]

Despite his success and his fame, Smith was bothered by the discrimination African Americans still suffered. With the support of other athletes as well as civil rights leader Martin Luther King, Jr., Smith called for a boycott of the 1968 Olympics. It did not seem to make sense to run for a country that did not give them equal rights. But when many other athletes refused to join the boycott, Smith and his supporters decided to attend, too. "I'll go on and try to win and stand up for what I believe in," he said.[2]

In Mexico City, at the semifinals of the Olympic 200, Smith clocked a decent 20.13. But as the race ended, he felt a sharp pain. "It was like a dart in my leg," he said. "I went down, not knowing where the next bullet was coming from."[3] It was not a bullet; it was an injured adductor muscle. A trainer pulled him up and packed his groin in ice. Two hours later, with yards of tape wrapped around his leg, he hoped he was ready for the final.

At the gun, he ran lightly to keep pressure off the inside of his thigh. But the leg did not hurt! So he took off. Eight long hard strides carried him past teammate John Carlos. As he crossed the finish line, his arms extended out from his sides and a smile swept across his face. In winning, he had set a world record of 19.83 seconds. Eighty thousand fans roared their approval.

But a few minutes later the cheers turned to jeers. At the medal ceremony, Smith and Carlos were not just wearing the customary warm-up suits. They wore black socks and no shoes, as a symbol of black poverty. Then, while the American national anthem played, they each raised one black-gloved clenched fist in a black power salute.

Because of their protest, both men were expelled from the Olympic Village. Most white Americans seemed to be shocked at the gesture. They thought the Olympic Games were not the proper place to make a protest. Some African Americans agreed.

But when he returned to the United States, Smith visited his father. "He looked right through me, stone silent. . . ." Then he reached for his son's hand. "I don't really know what happened," he said, "but what you did was right."[4]

Wyomia Tyus, the African-American woman who won the 100-meter dash in Mexico City, dedicated her gold medal to Smith and Carlos. Years later, she said, "What I did was win a track event. What they did lasted a lifetime, and life is bigger than sport."[5]

Since 1978, Smith has served as track and cross country coach at Santa Monica College in California.

TOMMIE SMITH

BORN: June 5, 1944, Clarksville, Texas.

HIGH SCHOOL: Central Union High School, Lemoore, California.

COLLEGE: San Jose State University.

MEDALS: Gold medal winner, 200-meter dash, 1968 Olympics.

HONORS: Inducted into USA Track and Field Hall of Fame, 1978.

By 1996, much of the country had forgiven Smith (right) and Carlos for their protest. They were chosen as two of the torch carriers for the games in Atlanta.

Internet Address

http://www.usatf.org/athletes/hof/smith.shtml

Eddie Tolan receives his gold medal for the 100-meter dash. Tolan edged fellow American Ralph Metcalfe by the slimmest of margins.

HIS VISION WAS SO POOR that he could not see without glasses. Being an African American during the early part of the twentieth century also meant that he faced intense discrimination. But none of that could stop Eddie Tolan from being a star quarterback at Cass Technical High School in Detroit, Michigan. Even though he only weighed 132 pounds, he once scored 6 touchdowns in a single game.

Tolan also became a track star. It was tough to run, because his glasses kept bouncing around, and sometimes even falling off. He solved that problem by taping them to his head. He was the Michigan state champion in both the 100- and 220-yard sprints.

After winning a scholarship to the University of Michigan, Tolan hoped to become a football star, but his size finally stopped him. By then, he was only five-feet seven-inches and 145 pounds. His football coaches convinced him he was not big enough to play college football. They told him to stick to track.

The little sprinter with the glasses taped to his head soon became a well-known figure. Fans across the country noticed that his jaw chewed gum almost as fast as his legs chugged down tracks. Tolan's skin color made him stand out even more. During the 1920s, the only other nationally known African-American sports stars were boxers.

Tolan set Big Ten Conference records in the 100- and 220-yard sprints. He also became the first runner to clock 9.5 seconds for the 100-yard dash. At the same time, he was earning excellent grades on his way to graduating from

Michigan. His goal was to become a doctor when his racing days were through.

But first he had to meet Ralph Metcalfe, another African American, in a pair of incredible races at the 1932 Olympics in Los Angeles. Japan's Takayoshi Yoshioka took the early lead in the 100-meter dash. Tolan passed him at 40 meters, but then Metcalfe took off. His finally caught his teammate at 80 meters, and the two men blazed side by side across the finish line in 10.3 seconds, tying for the world record.

Tolan and Metcalfe were so close that the judges could not decide who had won. It took several hours for a film of the race to be developed and examined. After careful viewing, the judges finally declared that Tolan had the gold medal. His margin of victory was just two inches!

The next day, Metcalfe beat everybody in the 200-meter preliminaries, but in the final, another American, Ralph Simpson, took the early lead. Tolan passed him with fifty meters to go, then stumbled and almost fell at the finish line. He still finished five or six feet ahead of Simpson. But what had happened to Metcalfe? He had surprised almost everybody by coming in third. When judges viewed the films, they discovered why. In a staggered start, Metcalfe had been directed to line up three or four feet behind the proper spot. Officials offered to rerun the race, but he refused. He said he was glad the Americans had swept the top three places.

Tolan was very proud of his Olympic triumphs. He was the first African-American athlete to win two gold medals. Newspapers called him the Midnight Express. Tolan said, "Men of color around the world were never before so stirred emotionally."[1]

He never became a doctor, because he could not come up with the money for medical school. Instead he worked as a physical education teacher in Detroit.

EDDIE TOLAN

BORN: September 29, 1908, Denver, Colorado.

DIED: January 30, 1967.

HIGH SCHOOL: Cass Technical High School, Detroit, Michigan.

COLLEGE: University of Michigan.

MEDALS: Gold medal winner, 100-meter dash, 1932 Olympics; Gold medal winner, 200-meter dash, 1932 Olympics.

HONORS: Inducted into USA Track and Field Hall of Fame, 1982.

Eddie Tolan won the gold medal in both the 100-meter and 200-meter dashes at the 1932 Olympics. He was the first African-American to win two gold medals.

Internet Address

http://www.usatf.org/athletes/hof/tolan.shtml

Chapter Notes

Henry Carr

1. Jack Olsen, "The Doves and Gongs of Tokyo," *Sports Illustrated*, October 19, 1964, p. 41.
2. John Underwood, "An Exuberant Finish in Tokyo," *Sports Illustrated*, November 2, 1964, p. 29.

Bob Hayes

1. Bob Hayes with Robert Pack, *Run, Bullet, Run* (New York: Harper & Row, 1990), p. 2.
2. Ibid., p. 21.
3. Ibid., p. 24.
4. Ibid., pp. 28–29.
5. Ibid., p. 25.

Jim Hines

1. Kenny Moore, "A Courageous Stand; in '68, Olympians Tommie Smith and John Carlos Raised Their Fists for Racial Justice," *Sports Illustrated*, August 5, 1991, p. 72.
2. Kenny Moore, "The Eye of the Storm: The Lives of the U.S. Olympians Who Protested Racism in 1968 Were Changed Forever," *Sports Illustrated*, August 12, 1991, p. 66.
3. Ibid.
4. Ibid.

Michael Johnson

1. Michael Johnson, *Slaying the Dragon* (New York: Regan Books, 1996), p. 18.
2. Ibid., p. 25.
3. Ibid., p. xiii.
4. Sam McManis, "Fastest, Greatest, Best—That's Michael Johnson," Knight-Ridder/Tribune News Service, August 2, 1996.
5. Ibid.
6. Johnson, p. xiv.

Carl Lewis

1. Franz Lidz, "Between Halves of a Football Game, Carl Lewis's Storied Career Came to a Close," *Sports Illustrated*, September 22, 1997, p. 26.
2. Jerry Izenberg, *Lincoln Library of Sports Champions* (Columbus, Ohio: Frontier Press Company, 1985), vol. 12, p. 120.
3. "Carl Lewis," *USATF On the Web*, n. d., <http://www.usatf.org/athletes/bios/lewis.shtml> (August 21, 1998).
4. David Wallechinsky, *The Complete Book of the Summer Olympics* (Boston: Little, Brown and Company, 1996), p. 14.

5. Ibid., p. 15.

6. Kenny Moore, "The Great Race: Carl Lewis Shattered the World Record in the Best 100-Meter Dash Ever Run," *Sports Illustrated*, September 2, 1991, p. 26.

7. Ralph Hickok, *Who's Who of Sports Champions* (New York: Houghton-Mifflin, 1995), p. 478.

Bobby Joe Morrow

1. David Wallechinsky, *The Complete Book of the Summer Olympics* (Boston: Little, Brown, and Company, 1996), p. 10.

Jesse Owens

1. Ralph Hickok, *Who's Who of Sports Champions*, (New York: Houghton-Mifflin, 1995), p. 614.

2. Rhussus L. Perry, "Fastest Runner in the World," Jesse Owens Trust.

3. Duff Hart-Davis, *Hitler's Games: The 1936 Olympics* (New York: Harper & Row, 1936), p. 239.

Charlie Paddock

1. Richard Schapp, *An Illustrated History of the Olympics* (New York: Alfred A. Knopf, 1967), p. 143.

2. David Wallechinsky, *The Complete Book of the Summer Olympics* (Boston: Little, Brown, and Company, 1996), p. 6.

3. Schapp, p. 176.

Tommie Smith

1. Kenny Moore, "A Courageous Stand: In '68, Olympians Tommie Smith and John Carlos Raised Their Fists for Racial Justice," *Sports Illustrated*, August 5, 1991, p. 64.

2. Pete Axthelm, "Boos and a Beating for Tommie," *Sports Illustrated*, January 29, 1968, p. 59.

3. Moore, p. 64.

4. Kenny Moore, "The Eye of the Storm: The Lives of the U.S. Olympians Who Protested Racism in 1968 Were Changed Forever," *Sports Illustrated*, August 12, 1991, p. 66.

5. Kenny Moore, "Wyomia Tyus: A Child of Jim Crow, She Refused to Run Second to Anyone," *People*, July 15, 1996, p. 109.

Eddie Tolan

1. "Eddie Tolan: Runner Sprinted into History Books," *Detroit Free Press freep/black history*, February 13, 1997, <http://www.freep.com/blackhistory/bio/qbio13.htm> (August 21, 1998).

INDEX